Sonnets

Sonnets

JOSEPH NICOLELLO

RESOURCE *Publications* · Eugene, Oregon

SONNETS

Resource Publications
An Imprint of Wipf and Stock Publishers
199 W. 8th Ave., Suite 3
Eugene, OR 97401

www.wipfandstock.com

PAPERBACK ISBN: 978-1-6667-5747-7
HARDCOVER ISBN: 978-1-6667-5748-4
EBOOK ISBN: 978-1-6667-5749-1

09/19/22

itinerarium mentis,
mysticum iter

And O what gravity sits upon me here
Indeed I am a fellow with something of the world upon my shoulders.

—JOAN MURRAY

I am turning toward a kind of aesthetic mysticism . . . When there is no
encouragement to be derived from one's fellows, when the exterior world
is disgusting, enervating, corruptive, and brutalizing, honest and sensitive
people are forced to seek somewhere within themselves a more suitable
place to live. If society continues on its present path I believe we shall see
the return of mystics as have existed in all the dark ages of the world. The
soul, unable to overflow, will be concentrated in itself. The time is not far
off when we shall see the return of world-sickness—beliefs in the Last Day,
expectation of the Messiah, etc. But all this enthusiasm will be ignorant of
its own nature, and, the age being what it is, can have no theological foun-
dation: what will be its basis? Some will seek it in the flesh, others in the
ancient religions, others in art; humanity, like the Jewish tribes in the desert,
will adore all kinds of idols. We were born a little too early: in twenty-five
years the points of intersection of these quests will provide superb subjects
for masters. Then prose (Prose especially, the youngest form) will be able to
play a magnificent humanitarian symphony.[1]

—GUSTAVE FLAUBERT

1. The reader may well ponder at this reference to prose in a volume of poetry. But this book, *Sonnets*, is in fact the postscript to a previous book of mine, entitled *Until the Sun Breaks Down*. One familiar with the end of that labyrinthine work shall recall the closing moments of the Dantean oratorio; the present work is a poetical analysis of the split second the protagonist of that work and the reader of it share upon completion of their respective tasks. For every poem in this volume is likewise a singular angle on the solitary second in question of William Fellows and Octavia Savonarola standing together in the cathedral. To give one example, consider the opening line of Sonnet LXIX in this light: a metaphor for the protagonist's early, adolescent devouring of European literature. Every angle is a dissection of the former's mind at that moment, dialectically converged with the reader's conscience. At the same time, no prior knowledge of that vast work is needed to read what follows.

I. VERLAINE IN PRISON

In his cement tent this sick prince observes
An invisible parade's citation,
Confused metaphor and designation,
Rust slept whence mouse utopia unnerves.
Barren is the absinthe moon, which tears swerve
With restrained clouds whose long indication—
Revelry suffers reanimation,
As he torn turns from mouse to servant, *Serve.*
"O Lord, pray why did thy command miss them"—
But then all their energies guide the mill
That grinds unliving bones, causality's
Behavior unto nervous system.
Reticular formations the damned kill,
Selected nervous circuits, morality.

II. I DOTH NOT FEAR, THOUGH THE EARTH SHOULD PERISH [VARIATION ON PS. 46:3]

Holy is the prisoner whose flesh turns
The gate of Heaven. For the king is gone,
Dead, and the queen swore sacral oath, its bond
Contended the murdered God. But then Burns
Adorned cobalt lambskin, apron discerned
At Osirian woods, some candidate upon
The threshold, that spirit imprisoned, conned,
Thrusts down approved histories. One thence learned
By the suicide of God, my oath, what
Milton meant about regicide, Satan's sun,
Divine repetition and destruction
of the inner citadel, bells in rut,
Tonsured storming that Plotinian One,
Blood in watering bucket, seduction.

III.

Perishing of the nation by false light,
its relation to the material
substance of the walls, light imperial
and true, with filters through this porous flight
against shadows permeating tight,
merging, transfiguring the serial.
Corporate goddesses, arterial
Vitruvian transparent rendered flight
Thus compositional, to now reveal
Geometrical law as principle
that guides their creative intuition,
the precious jewel of geometry seals
our calendrical fate, its lethal pull
on prisoners, desperate with omission.

IV.

That lethal safety all tyrants cherish
Beyond Sodom and beyond Gomorrah
Render alchemies of finance perished
Harness vests and suicide menorahs.
There is no change save objects parallel
To the estrangement of essence, Being,
Ease begets comfortably fatal Hell,
The hollow garbs and scripts feign unseeing.
Pyramidal players, bought and sold like
Prostituted gazetteers, hand grenades,
And seers blinded by linguistic Fourth Reich's
Propaedeutic, more cerebral arcades.
Persistent seduction, destruction past
And present; therefore I say *safety last*.

V.

Only uniform mortal veils arise
Despite eternal wanderings, insights,
When hangmen, faithfully platonic, quite
Skilled in procuring August ram that dies.
We should be horrified by death, and yet
Further horrified by wasting our lives;
Severance from public opinion strives
For nothing more than unveiling its set
Ways at which point greatness may, can commence.
Take by storm the desert of the real, whence
You have destroyed that poisoned root regret.
Born to lose, Pascallan with our safe bet,
There are no liberal arts tomorrow,
Breaking and entering the soul rape's sorrow.

VI.

Existence was the longing not to die.
Every last golden grim particle fact
Recaptured by the slides that at last cracked
Beneath avalanching despair, tears dried
Albeit swallowed. Graveside flowers hide
Nature's unconcealment alas, alack,
Replacement paralyzed by torture wracks,
Replenishment lost in heavy truths, lies:
That lonely place, where even language fails.
Memories of a first encounter turns
To cruelty, incomprehension, lost
Are the days of automatism's pails
Filled up with the waters of peace, which burn
In memory instead of soothe this frost.

VII. MUSEUM OF REVOLUTION

Men in costumes counting money, symbols
Crisp and withered, bottles of soap, tissue,
By the box north and south, starlight issued
In cardboard paper. It is time to lull
Oneself to sleep wine, pills: sharply null.
The old man says to his mind: "I miss you."
Calendrical exhaustion, years wished through,
Garments folded, safe locked, closet near full,
The evening prayers no longer matter now
That despair came knocking just this past May.
It happened in a violent way, the vow
Broken clean in half, the sky steel-blue, gay,
Procession canceled by rain, lightning, plough;
Constellation myths, cape draped, night and day.

VIII.

The accent delirium that loses
Its languageless sun there, the black sun-itself,
Strapped like a captured criminal. Black Guelph
Once lodged weeping in a well with the muses,
Tunnel tint of sound, with matchbook and fuses
Redirects blue-green burning sphere to Gothelf,
His shelved portrait thus becomes itself a shelf,
"Vampiric drunk-boats," sing dispossessed ruses,
"Scream, weep, falling sun! Othered, demurred, wracked!
"Thou art the essence of interruption,
"The purity of nonbeing! Crawl, cracked!
"Ye concept—force, ye thought, ye risen sin!
"Rise by fall, progress to digress—alack!
"Perished son of the morning—lo!—begin."

IX. ISAIS SAWED IN TWO

I invoke the spirit of the end,
Absolute negativity enthroned,
Before angels of death, their canyon bones,
Collected at Satan's temple. I bend
The heart's needle, listen: Thou shall not mend
This broken road of space; now war's enthroned,
Infinite war, mind and land, last seeds sewn
Across atrophied soil. Now *bow*, I lend
You life as long as ye kneel; this switchblade
World of compromise is settled. Ashes
To ashes, libraries of stone, dust, made
To overflow with blood, secretion, flashes
Of a whipped chorus-regicide on ice.
At this thus I lunged, not thinking twice.

X. SATAN'S WALTZ

Western witchcraft is a forlorn disgrace,
From the way it speaks and stares at screens she
Is a physiologic nightmare free
From sanity and introspection. Case
After case of pills, divorce, no true trace
Remains across her amputated sea
Of turnstiles, turnstile amputations, we
Hear screams within her downhill motor race
To the pit of deception, delusion,
A sickly maze of three inverted persons:
the liar, the imbecile, and the great
enabler. Darkness of the world's fusion,
Where time's run out, in any faint version
of her specter of simulated fate.

XI. OUTLINES OF PYRRHONISM

My dream woman puts me out of my vile
Last hollow love round the sundry corner,
Veiled nations, candlelit like some mourners,
Like justice, both phantoms of a dream while
Those Harvard 1969 turnstiles,
Archaeologies that did adorn her
Pinecone breastplate laden with that former
Parental straightjacket cut down, beguiled.
With Edward Taylor seek not temporal
Trends but Scotus, Gothicism heavy.
She says there was never the perfect man
Round the bend, justice's vacant portal
Splintery pandemonium, my levy—
Those phantoms of thy dream commence quicksand.

XII. THUS WANTING IN DESPAIR TO BE ONESELF

An objective ontology of sin,
Defying defiance's forfeitures,
Leads to sapped lead's repulsion of regret
That no juridical pills can save, win.
Yet we're here where eternal gates begin,
Precited syncretic distinguishment,
The air-conditioned nightmare's cobwebbed vent
For frames of light that fall away within.
Chanting mobs vault preordained bottled tar,
The grate flood's antipathetical jar.
The saving power's in the lyric cloak,
But nobody knows why—no ancient, nay,
Scholars, whores, no—philosophers like smoke,
Just vanish in multivariate ways.

XIII. LOCKED HORIZONS

Cerulean surge, golden foam forming
At labor's nocturne, some harrowed comet,
My alchemical Latin hours—yet
This be where bent love's broken, adorning
Sacred hatreds, predetermined, forming
insect masses clash, compute grave vomit.
Vials of evaporation beget
The wires of death that stamp, bind thy mourning.
Bondage's discovery, quartermaster,
Drinking rubied alley port, but faster,
Mutable cosmos that fit in one's throat,
Twelve propagandists burnt inside the mote.
Ecclesiastical architecture,
Mutinies my porcelain conjectures.

XIV. LAURA LIVING

Laura living, giving way to last page
Of a book she denies writing with grave shame,
A thing far from foundation degrees. Blame
For sale, some tabernacle nonsense, rage
Codified, diluted, swallowed sand-cage.
Thine paralytic memories enflamed,
Like mother's cigarette lighter whose fame
In forestry and laundromat adage,
Brought Laura to the forefront of failure.
Nothing dreams, but misinterpretations
Turn her grey panel door to sooty lock,
That secret place where she hides from jail pure
and simple. Thoughtless frame, variations,
some faded friend's picnic at hanging rock.

XV.

The halls of philosophy are sterile,
Windswept, filled with frauds foreign, domestic.
Security, ease unfold, the rest thick
With a hatred of truth, spirits feral
And destroyed by corporations. Peril
Says—no, forget peril—all is lost, sick
When sandglass perturbations lent vents thick
Like chorus orgies of the state settled,
Without declaring who among us shall
Suffer the little children, left to this
Veritable factory line of mind,
Wherein external cash tender corrals
Corporation's whist, Athens dismissed,
Roman ledgers shredded unto thought-crimes.

XVI. BLACK HORSE ALLEY: SUNDAY, AUGUST, WHITMAN

A person who will apologize for wrongs he didn't
commit is capable of all sorts of terrible things.[1]

Artistic creation from great pain sees
Beauty and the laws derived to govern,
Immutable values of false love burnt
Transcendental order, theology,
Resurrects hollow men, thy truth frees
From coercion unleavened. Our dove learnt
O'er the tyranny of heaven, earned
Solitude's ocean of light, ray of seas,
Crystal ships, white nights. Santayana pulled
down, entombed with soil, crumpled foil, veins full
of Moloch's concoctions, deception's wool
set against torn-out eyes of effectual,
continental pits, intellectual
gentrification reigns inceptual.

1. *A Brighter Summer Day* (Criterion Collection) 1:11:05.

XVII.

Nonexistence taking form, lullaby
Of all the screenlit eyes, cloth erasure,
Subject and predicate of nothing pure,
Fascism's nature, that vial zombified.
From their computer chairs the good men tried,
They tried in pews and recliners, manure
That makes the mushroom grow: there is no cure,
As pierced subjects proceed to save the sky.
Nonexistence taking form, shaped like a pill,
Orange cylinders execute thy will,
Clerics of death dig at digital hill.
Wailing child, with rattle and cloth well-worn,
Mother deflated, out of milk and corn,
They walked in line, nothingness taking form.

XVIII. WE DEPORT OURSELVES IN OTHER RESPECTS

Ideas, ideas alone, are real,
The keystone of gothic vaults
Typologized, Dionysian salt
And honey, a vision of heaven steals
John of Salisbury and midnight oil, peels
Back that myth which shall sequester each fault.
For the course is set; and this valid weal
Of all dialogic wounds, ranging from
Ancient constellation myths to the myths
That spark, maintain genocides. Ideas grieve
not because they are not unlike myths, dumb
Oxen of the sun. Rather, fittest piths
believe that they believe that they believe.

XIX. MY TROUBLES WRAPPED IN DREAMS TO NO AVAIL

Emblazoned brides to-be unbox the fair,
Plastic flowers in their hair, malnourished
Nowhere but by multicolored eyes. Fished
Out of parish guilds, disconsolate lairs,
Handling bagged goldfish with surveilled care,
Digital lockets and some four-leafed wish,
Whispering of sin, nightfall, mother's dish
Of this and that before escaping, air
That spells out light sparks of summer reason.
Journeying out across the sleeping town,
Mingling with crickets and shadows so long,
When at once another mental season
Overtakes her direction, breaks her down,
Little girl lost in cosmos sings her song.

XX. RITTENHOUSE SQUARE

But ah—is that a road, or forest path?
A ferry for Gabriola in March?
Forest murmurs, fire music, grape-wrath:
Ecstatic spirit overtakes her, Arch
And fifth. Flower-lady at the fountain
Exhaling harpsicords of light and wine;
I bring her monastic psalter, mountain
Book of Kells. And like flappers less refined
Than hanged with quicksand-sleep we shall journey
To the end of the recalcitrant night.
Hand in hand, body to body, tourneyed
Promises snap like brittle sticks alight.
One of us must know if this be the road;
Till then together give and take the load.

XXI. STOPPING AT THE PHILADELPHIA IRISH MEMORIAL ONE MORNING IN JULY

Believe nothing now except everything,
And something less than matter hinders thee,
Cornfield decay, the tower's brevity
Entombed by cruelty. I hath seen rings
Around the moon, where a haloed saint sings
No more. Now rich are poor, poor dead, and free
From starving summer cannibals like me,
Free from media and politicians,
Their siblings pilgrimaging, struck with shock,
Whispering prayers through their beaded fingers.
The famine wrecked visible conditions
Scarce sundry flowers withstood like a rock,
Their spark lives in I and thou; it lingers.

XXII. MARATHONS OF HEROD: AN INTERLUDE

The First Lady is one of Hegel's plants,
The dummy another lovely Herod,
Innocents of Bethlehem at crusade,
Condemn the eternality of the golden calf.

Cease skeleton-fillings of tectonic,
Cosmographia Munster, Silvestris,
Craving for light, gallery & triforium,
Placed between the nave arcades and clerestory.

Austerity of unostentatious forms!
The poisoned oak that makes up
Scientism's cradle, breaks down at
Reinstated archivolts, God's nocturnal altar.

My kairotic Thierry of Chartres,
Who saw the mystery of the Trinity,
As geometrical demonstration,
Monad and dyad with God and matter,

I was there when all the politicians died,
Teeth torn out like page of tint red Macrobius,
And we praised architectural
Symphonies all our days, & th'
Cosmos as a work of architecture!

XXIII. PREPARATIONS FOR LATIN MASS, ADVENT

She was called to greater unconcealment,
Two sanctuary spheres: Bonaventure's
Blessed Virgin, Christ's Nativity (myrrh
And frankincense with Rachmaninoff). Lent's
Memory, that God shall love her, boughs bent
By familial hatreds. But she fused lure
And lyre: profound mystical insight pure,
an irrepressible tendency sent
to mystify: Dormition of the Virgin.
That Athenian clave unto St. Paul
She loved & believed in the heart's time bomb,
That loss of faith in faith, could call no surgeon,
Dreams snapped like twigs, that echoing footfall,
The hermitage within sang her its psalm.

XXIV. WASHINGTON SQUARE

In days past I could raise a plastic glass
To the future, to your eyes, to this lawn;
Washington Square, where we had loved, laughed, fawned,
Over the cosmic implications, lass,
Of old me, wiry and whiskey-scorched, class
Discarded in the name of brighter pawns,
& the masonic checkerboard Sorbonne.
Your pressed felt dress, all mine to crumple fast
When the dusk melts into nocturnal breath.
But it begins, began, here in the park,
Younger and unaware of things that come,
Their shape, this wincing way of powdered wreaths,
Autumn leaves, memories, ascendant larks,
Full moon mouths, soil pressed, seed buried with thumb.

XXV.

The string of life unravels at the seams,
For the filched import knows not what it means,
When lovers scream and wrench and lunge like fiends,
Onto something I seek not in my dreams,
Nor in my waking life—no wife, no themes
Of marriage shall serve. All those minds picked clean
By the nostalgia industry demean
Poet-philosophers in smithereens,
And for the sake of what? The lion sleeps
Alone in the jungle tonight, his cohorts
Having promulgated scarce contempt, got
Thrown into the slaughterhouse of creeps,
Filled with film and cantankerous retort,
The world is hopeless but one's craft is not.

XXVI. FIELD RECORDING: SPRUCE STREET HARBOR PARK

The telescope of early times, our line
of signified horizons; progress comes
not with mind but hand. Iniquity's sum
of oblivion, registered, refined
at Hamlet's mill, scatters terminal brine,
the terror and the poppies and some rum.
I hear women's voices, flies at mad dung
Of screens—udders gawk, death knells unrefined.
Precession of the Equinoxes, that
Equinoctial sun occupies, at
Zodiacal constellation myth free,
Elusively fluid, relinquished.
We turn to Chaos, when law, wish,
And knowledge was serious poetry.

XXVII. TREE OF DEATH

Time proceeds in cycles of flowering
and decay, depicting the bleak forces
that hath overtaken cosmos, spent courses,
Fixed stars, hidden counsels, struggle's showering,
That which is, was, faced with itself cowering
as-not. Sing history's hidden forces,
their adventive barbarism, horses
of despondency, nightmares towering,
Three lovers entwined to the bitter end.
Wearing cloaks of funerary linen,
Sickle reigns of Saturn soon forgiven,
Saeturnus, Saturnus, heliacal doubt,
Justification reigns, tyrants thus mend
Themselves in the delirium of gout.

XXVIII. JUDGMENT OF THE NATIONS

The sound of waiting buries bliss alive,
Memory's record sleeves become blank slates.
I see Satan fall like lightning, arrived
Thought trammeled neath the furies and the fates;
Saints and blesseds standing, chanted, gilded, true:
Thou shalt set the volume of the evil one to mute.
Man canst fill woman with life *and* death through
Seed; Man may be filled solely with death's lute.
When donator is condemned by nature's
Receiver, it's time for empire to die.
All complex cultures collapse, poor creatures;
Still it is agonizing every time.
There is no progress but posterity;
There is no future for the home called free.

XXIX. MARCH OF THE PEASANTS

H.D.'s grave obscured by broken lantern,
Apuleius staggering through long dark
trail, ressentiment Basilica stark
was an image of heaven. Light burns,
its construction's manual labor turns,
canst relate to the spiritual ark
and process of edification's lark
ascending. But no, my poet, that Kern
Druidic sightings, Caesarian lore,
Burnt to crisp with simplicity's mirror,
Dan Healy at Shelley's side, pamphlets bought
Like thine, H.—Complex societies brought
Marble phallus, words like revolving doors.
whose field of death is thy past and future.

XXX. VOYAGING OUT, THE FOUR-SEASON'D MERCHANT

Cathedral foyer, candle-box wood,
With winter words that accent like flushed reeds,
The beauty of the inner man proceeds—
My last bias, the mentally ill, could
Between theologian and artist should
Who through my Roman-Celtic anomy
Operate not with trends but with gods freed
From chrysalis, extinction stilted stood.
Obedience or nothing, whence the tare
illuminates voiceless builders' intellect,
Makes moral & artistic powers right,
Descent from Dionysiac grace, squared
penultimate order that resurrects.
My light put out, whence I put out the light.

XXXI. DAMNATION

Once more they were left with sedition sheer,
As the last chain-link of reason, Van Eyck
Ablaze, mutinous museum dreams break
Down in surrendered nights, rape-machines leer,
Thucydidean vision equips seers
Semonides, Polybius, earthquake
Seasons of the soul, with a brutal rake.
Empedocles in pocket I kneel-leer.
Causal being reflects itself in
the completion of thought; arrowed verse is
borne sublime, made ill by disloyalty.
Their gods as comprehension of real sin,
unfolding of free will, nearness now his
to predestination, should gods decree.

XXXII. CHRISTMAS ORATORIO

Summon me at will, and I shall shield thee.
Calamity sparks resolution wise
to rebuild, in a manner once surmised
psychically impossible. Tilting she
absorbed his final heartbeat, broke free,
Running lost in the future of streets, lies,
Factories of crucified dreams collide,
When she set about at sunrise's sea.

Transform my platonic hearths of heather,
Adorned with halo of peacock feathers,
None free nor brave, torn trampled flowers
frozen stiff enslaved, and terrorized hours,
Fumes of peppermint pine tree like tonic
Take us from telos to cosmogonic.

XXXIII. GATES OF LIGHT

The first flowering of scholasticism,
Forged credentials set down the essence of prisms
Imaginative & didactic—Being's
Foundation ceremony, serpent's fleeing.
Some obscure feast day grandmother would have loved,
white-black sacerdotal. The wings of the dove,
The queen's two bodies revealed through smoke and guns,
Nothing less than Saturn's late devoured sons.
Concord and homogeneity nurture
Architects of theology, blessed searchers,
Who drink from the real chalice of salvation,
Architectural reconciliation.
The children of yearning's internal fencing,
He leadeth them at the hour of incensing.

XXXIV. CHORAL INTERLUDES

A.
Their destruction of humanistic dreams,
For silver globe's worldwide banquet of blood,
Acceptance or refusal Light serene,
Quell or enable this internal flood.
Awareness of the victim, crystallized
in the symbol of the cross, sciences
that reject origins doth carve out eyes,
Assuage vague danger's appliances.
Until they're cross-examined by the gods
Salvation through Dionysius takes
The call of priests of earliest rites, rods,
Initiations transposed in silver flakes.
Likewise as gods in death beneath, below,
Beyond, above, Egyptian undertow.

B. The Cosmic Event of Hierogamy
To the little Valentinian girl lost,
Thy gods—priests or guardians—shan't turn to frost.
Priestly judges of the next world (Egypt) brought out
Into not-posthumous realms the sought route.
For verticality's dismemberment-gods
Orphic rite's omophagic salvation plods
Her mythic prison of the body, filling
A bottomless pit with water, gods willing
Apocalypse in metempsychosis lifts
Analogous descents, funerary drifts.

Mediations, sacrificial monarchies,
Taurine attribute and even-victim sees
Goat and ram of epopteia, a pledge
Of lasting objectual possession's hedge.

C. For Vico
Death and terror of raw plurality, flesh
Known to Clement of Alexandria, fresh
As an ear of corn reaped in silence, labyrinth
Mythologem. Object-victim anomy, Cynth's
Twin towers Jachin and Boaz, no, narthex
and tribune, that turmoil of awe and dread sex
Ne'er did live up to. Vortex assuaged,
None happy as baby birds eating garbage.
Homer's man doth not see in himself the source
of his decisions. We go back further, coarse,
to Protagoras, to comprehend the thick
smoke of hours. Sapphic Being through exilic,
Pindaric weaving of the chaplets. Despise
all stadiums with thy bright internal eyes.

D. Stadium Ruins
The transitory world partakes in divine
Form, and it is my task to make this known, thine.
I can take thy verbal stones and later wounds,
But I cannot take concealment's obtunds
Lost to greater prurient posterity.
The orgy of the crowd declines before me,
Digital pillars of dust and excrement,
Passing through into oblivion long spent.
All their evil days of screens and vile chanting,
The dogs of Gomorrah transfixed and panting,
Who through deceptive purpose suicidal,
I waged Pindaric war against the idols.
Muted chorus, bound by fractal stalemated
Limbo, in particle showers sedated.

XXXV. THE TRUE SOVEREIGN, MELANCHOLY

Ferlinghetti's season of conversion,
As I read Charles Olson *Maximus* through
Sunday summer alley's Letters Persian.
Love's outdoor café thrown off bus too,
The 38 in fact, stoned, wrecked, lighter,
A smoking skull of morphine whiskey blues.
I always found Lawrence a poor writer,
Like affirmative action hires, like clues,
Simulated recognition, stone halls,
False symposiums. If light ceased to shine
All life would be evaporated, all
Epistemology of souls refined.
The Areopagite demolishes
the profane schools' temporal polishes.

XXXVI. THE COMFORTS OF DESTRUCTION

Nothing must be better than anything,
Higher symmetry, paperback Li Po,
You ask me nothing, except you see, though,
Stylized sightless in the bonfire flings
Regarding essence, loneliness, a ring
Around [Lucifer's son's] finger, that throws
Molten light into that furnaced past so
Slow to swallow whole tablatures that bring
History says naught to the tender lush,
With easel stick, cassock, and fresh wine jug
We know we were right at the beginning,
Body-to-body, no religious rush,
When morals were for criminals, to tug
And pull my daisy, glorious sinning.

XXXVII.

Thou hate the children of a higher Lord,
Becoming Hell yourself, revolting cogs
In a wheel that spares thee least of all, frogs
At swim in two birds-nests of boiling stored
Up chemical water taproot, accord
Them weary lens, historicity fogs
Feeling retreat yet moving forward, logs
Of hand-carved raping angels canst afford
To suffer little demons unto thee.
Promises invisible and elsewise,
The coin itself is cratered inferno.
Thou hate thy own creations, wild and free,
Leaving to politicians to surmise
That atlas of thy history hitherto.

XXXVIII. DIALECTIC, DIALOGIC

Reaction is that society-mind,
"I like this, indeed I'll like this too thus
"The masses agree, whereby I ought find,
"Reality derived from consensus."
Holy living, holy dying's pearl fences,
"I will not rebel just to rebel, give
"The Lord all, no matter consequences;
"Tell holy Truth, rather than lie and live."
This blessed accord is offered for one
And all, whilst metaphysical poets'
Sundry eyes thence beheld the Triune Son,
& revelatory nature showed it.
Sanctuaries heavenward built to last,
Connection with the Carolingian past.

XXXIX. MEANWHILE THE WORLD HATH BECOME PROSAIC

Whereby the church fails in its threefold
Task, mystical and liturgical mold,
Heaven's image, Celestial City,
From burnt soil of broken crypt to pity—
Offering's political popery,
Chain of black gravity, no hope for me,
Razed pews, transliterated command ploys,
Silence lost (silence is the sand of noise).
Apse adorned with the Christ of majesty
surrounded by his heavenly court free
in the eternity of truth I crave
an eternal School of the Heart to save
Inward heavenly sanctuary stores,
Churchlike edifice with tall open doors.

XL. *PARADISUS CLAUSTRALIS*

My love's garments atop mahogany,
Melancholic Magdalene engraving
Where all are saved there is thus no saving
Sewing the one, the many, and the three,
I must despise all fanatics equally
Here where the world of the senses hath no place,
Where there is nothing new and truth is disgraced,
Accept everything except truth's frequency.
The sacrifice of comfort is sanctified,
Some deprecated ostentatious buildings.
Wooden women look up lost to fish-hat rings,
Ill-bred, poor judgment in those rank-and-file
aesthetics. Mill-slaves can't comprehend
languished terror's all that's up around the bend.

XLI. AS FOR MY KINGDOM, TIS NOT OF THIS WORLD

That is no attic madwoman, nor entombed
confessor but Carolingian widow womb
Wide, whose solemn language transcends imagery,
The Mystery of the Incarnation frees,
And is and was the light that illuminates
the world. Her vision of the eucharistic
sacrament as divine light, a near mystic
transfiguring the darkness of matter hates
Saturn's six consistent applications gaze,
Lithophane vestiges traverse oblong bays,
She shall leave behind quaint sense-experience,
To perceive divine archival recompence
Of ultimate reality esteemed more,
Precocity at sumptuous golden door.

XLII. INTERROGATION OF PATOCKA

Marked off vertically by stringcourse, they pray.
Expurgated Romanesque gives way
To interior daybreak's martyrdom,
They're coming for he who'd speak the truth—run!
No, I shall not run—here I think, enthroned,
Vitruvius taught how to give thine own
atrium with octave ratio, bays
of the aisle side. The lifeworld, its rays
Divined through myth amd violence, Croix-rose
cosmic symphony, interweaving those
two spheres the satanic ilk cannot take
from one, be it me or St. Ambrose. Make
ambrosial therefore all thy dying hours:
Genocide's safety-whispers push forth flowers.

XLIII. THE HOLLOW HEAD

When she emulated Saint Ignatius
Studying Latin in Paris altered,
Across winter fields walking, her mind faltered
By the cadence of abandoned farms thus
Cornfield and the skeletons of both bus
And blackberry bushel. Off to Walter
Hilton at my lodge, Tennyson, psalter
By fresh-cut firewood. Friends make no fuss
In their last days, whence they're filled with real love,
As I was infused by my professor.
That was the snowclad afternoon, the dove
Of spirit in Tennyson's Lady, ah—bless her!
She there spoke to us, herself Shalot of
Country field campus, my last confessor.

XLIV. METAPHYSICAL DIGNITY AT SCAFFOLD

Representative geometry their
Vision of heaven's shapes, above all square,
Specialized secrets of medieval lodge,
Equilateral triangles and auge,
Acoustic qualities echo solemn
Science of good modulation, columned
Simple arithmetical ratios,
Secure dignity's adagio.
Audible echoes behold Heaven-Earth,
Prohibition's therapeutic hearse,
Exclusion of all imagery except
painted crucifixes, beads, ornaments,
Pilgrimage, devout lives incited thrice,
An image and foretaste of paradise.

XLV. EMBERS OF PENANCE

Catechetic experience impinged
Upon both monument and culture, singed,
Raked embers, threshold leading from the cries
Of life to the eternity that lies
beyond it. Byzantine mosaic slain
dost sing my tree of wooden clogs, its rains,
Rags lit with scarlet Osiris,
Ra, El, conquests of Cyprus and Isis.
Two small female figures, venerated
Wise and foolish virgins, crenelated
Edifice's caped cloak. Creation free,
Cities of imperceptibility.
Lucas Cranach the Elder baffles thee;
Yet he and thou make perfect sense to me.

XLVI. AGAINST THE AVALANCHE OF PARROT-WISDOM [BEAUTY AS THE SPLENDOR OF ONTOLOGICAL PERFECTION]

Bright objects break and out comes perfection,
Divinations of the True Creator,
Gray-green eyes reflect cosmos' election,
Gnosis as light, most noble of that stored
natural phenomenality, that
approximation to pure form's Beauty
is no mere value or insect all fat,
Numb, with concept-privilege. But through Me
The radiance of truth, that splendor made
Now essence whole, of ontological
perfection dispensed with ill-bred uncouth,
Proustian azure stones. And razing Hades,
Exorcised sacrificial chronicles,
Truth is more sacred, and death is the truth.

XLVII. IN DEFIANCE OF DEFIANCE

Severed herd matrix, random matrices,
I stand within labyrinth theophanies,
Mutual contradiction, God stages,
Interposes images between ages,
Him and us, kindled desires to ascend,
From a world of mere shadows that doth bend
Images, holier contemplation,
And Divine Light's constant coronation.
Confusion in created things dissolves
Before the first law of analogy,
Manifestations, various degrees
Images, vestiges, shadows of my
Creator's right hand extend grace, revolve,
At the cathedral portal this child cries.

XLVIII. FORM IS THE GOLDEN-LIGHTED STATION

New insight demands emancipation.
Music and architecture are sisters,
Umbilical breasts of eggy blisters,
Lenten pilgrim candles as oblation.
Architecture is endless creation,
Harmony, all ye artistic cisterns
Observe vessel-laws of numbered nations,
A roman city gate's last oblation,
Roaring ocean waves, birdsong, join seraphs
At Big Sur hermitage, as children laugh,
I turn to liturgical hymnody,
Ultimate peace, grace sufficient for thee,
Scaffold sent out for the acrylic lush,
Incensed Latinity, confession'l plush.

XLIX. THE PHENOMENON OF LOVE NEEDS FURTHER

Without the clear principate of number,
The cosmos would to chaos return,
Distrusting worlds of images discerned,
Whilst venerating absolute lumber,
Validity's mathematical slumber,
Relationships of monochord at burned
Intervals, divisions on a string learn,
Analogic precepts, sacral tumblers,
The illusion of perfection. For God
is a blasphemer, with his imperfect
Perfections; & Man's demiurgic, no
doctrine needed. The unconscionable rod
of Los, Lawrence, Aaron, that resurrects,
created through neglected self-defense.

L. THE FATE OF THE MIND MUST BE DESTRUCTION

The distinction between form and function
Hath vanished, the independence of form
from function hath fallen away reborn,
splendor of the city, pure gold junctions.
like to clear glass. That dazzling compunction's
Glitter of ancient basilica once sworn
Resplendent with jarred dust, lost silver torn
Columns, architrave, mental destruction,
Consolation of sepulchral structures,
For the slain prophets' tangible remains,
Dispersed by sacred geometricians,
Retaliatory space that ruptures
The geometrization of a sand grain,
Its optical value makes magicians.

LI. GNOSTIC RECIPROCATE

Ornamentation subordinated
To structural patterns, vault ribs and shafts
Support, determinate this wounded raft
Of an aesthetic system. Thus fated,
The observ'd laws of numbers now slated
For deconstruction. Hence the sexton laughs,
As in some decades historians shall craft
Inquiries on why those concerned with past
Slavery were not concerned with slavery
of the present moment, and it is because
of the myth that only past knavery
is legitimate, economic flaws
rather than justice, with their vile slave-made
check mark shoes, eye-phones, reason to evade.

LII. IT IS BOREDOM, NOT LOVE, THAT CONQUERS ALL

A shallow, transparent shell, one last prayer,
Continuous sphere of light, foil warm,
Luminously behind all tactile forms.
In the Gothic window, nothing compares,
To the solid elements of layers,
Tracery that floats, thy vision adorns
The luminous window's pattern is sworn
To the end of civilization rare,
Voiceless perpetuity is decay,
Dramatically articulated light,
That instinctual renunciation,
Predicates of consolation give way,
The culture of life gives way to guilt's right,
The suicide of culture and nation.

LIII. MASONS, CARPENTERS, AND OTHER CRAFTSMEN

An age of great fairs' ratiocinations,
Rabelaisian transformers stalking,
No fair without feast and no more talking,
Religious souvenirs, quashed oblations,
Devotional objects' indications,
Small leaden images of gawking
Nuns on strong beer with Our Lady walking
O'er fields of translucent invocations,
Of the riotous emotions gulped,
Devout attachment to basilica,
Amsterdam's animated port merchants,
Who slept under cathedral portals' pulp,
Certain parts of the crypt, gathered in the
Church itself, waiting to be hired freelance.

LIV. NOTES FROM SEVEN AGAINST POPE FRANCIS

Take it this placeless numinosity,
Process and progress are both blasphemies,
That demythologize the mind to freeze
Immediacy down on drenched bent knee
Redemption from thinking pied distraction,
Our destruction's all there is to action,
Political religion's subtraction,
Of the threshing floor's phallic infraction.
Pilgrims' cultivating soil fleeced these
Roses of light, lights of rose, transitioned
this creature toward God. Borne of constructive
Language is desecration's species,
Solitude's espousal, form, and mission,
But geometric precedence won't give.

LV. HYMN TO NOVALIS

He dreamt of ornament as well as order,
Cosmic temple as Platonic world soul,
Mixt with the Holy Ghost's creative whole,
Ordering effects on matter borders,
Melodic consonance's recorder,
That directs the reader not to sheer toll
But to the divine assistance that Rolle
In constructing mine own Samson's warder.
The illumination of their souls by
Visions of divine harmony is breath
Reflected in material artworks.
Though I am seditious when powers tried,
Neglect Polybius and die the death
of tyranny which is hatred, wrath, and murk.

LVI. THE MASS PSYCHOSIS THAT NOW GRIPS THE WORLD

That analogical theology
Is a stained-glass window, I doubt it not.
Their minds were blinded, forfeited to rot,
The ashen synagogue's dichotomy.
God is right there, not in work making free,
But through Incarnation and wheeler's pot,
Veils at once shrouding and revealing Lot's
Pillar of salt eternal. Were it me,
Those ineffable bonds, calcareous
Deposits, would abdicate cultures long
Defined by renunciation. Once free,
Until we changed definitions various
of human perfection, to mere swan song—
Mystical element's catastrophe.

LVII. THE ETERNAL IN ITS DIALECTIC

Communal ideal disregards the saint,
Renounced comprehension of viable,
Renunciation made reliable,
Manipulatable well-being paints
Admonition's expectable restraints,
Predicates of consolation made full.
It has been acknowledged, this mixture wool
Of cowardice and courage worn with taint,
The pope and his sons thus participate
in the panged, pitiful dissolution,
of their cultural functions. Decay's prime
motive must be sovereign exception's hate
that permeates with stiff Rosicrucian
hands, neither beautiful nor sublime.

LVIII. SACRED ARCHITECTURE

There is no world, nay, nothing but ladder,
Ladder of divine ascent, my two-edged
Sword of death and salvation, prayer wedged
Into the wall of crocodiles sadder
Who sought anguish to find sweet rest madder
Than the sweetness of sorrow. The priest pledged,
Temporality ordains a full-fledged
Literature, that God wills the sadder,
Tragic sense of life, a hermeneutic
Circle true to love's yearn therapeutic,
Against oblivion, which cheats me right
Out of my hero's ineffectual
Transfiguration, this long textual
Night my last memory of sacral light.

LIX. TRAGICALLY THE BOOKSTORES LOSE THEIR CHARM (INTERLUDE)

Cancer of the head, cancer of the mind,
I lost track of his demon's clenched foibles.
Columns of books enclosed them saturnine,
Now unlike the child Jesus's toy full
With something other than dreams colloidal,
Rigid limits, illustrative concerns,
Chameleon corporatism, Ubu Roi's pills
No longer work on taciturn interns.
Months of hard rain, where once devout fire burned.
What then is prayer, but talking to oneself,
Through vinyl dust tattoos that once seemed learned
It's predetermined, what makes it to shelf,
Enlightenment's wake, rectangular faces,
Worshippers of shadows make their cases.

*

Subordinated harmony befell,
Confused from conception, musical terms'
True beauty, visible harmony tells
The icon to partakes in texture firm,
Recurrent iconoclastic waves yearn,
Anchored metaphysic reality,
Serpentine spirit that stitches and churns
Out the window's bath of light like a sea,
Poverty of spirit's theology.

Musical consonances' visual
Proportions created by man thus free,
Partake of a sacred residual
Concord that transcends premeditation,
Waves shall break, relics of conflagration.

LX. PURITANS

O dessicate, wand'ring mountain lots,
Ghosted suburban knots of forestry,
You who can't let the angels sing to thee,
Wandering forsaken shopping malls not
Thinking of things you could explain: shot
After shot, the bottle's boring false glee,
Van Gogh's ear set in cardboard dumpster free
From the days like circling crows begot,
Of manifest desolation's highway.
None understand, none last, none care, none know,
The agony of walking round buildings,
Surrounded by lovers in arms all gay,
And baleful echo-laugher, black snow,
Horror's sky, streaked solicitude's gildings.

LXI. REPROBATION

As the holy relics were like armors,
Evaporated perils six and three,
The disappearance of the sacristy,
Made them forget about kidnapped farmers.
Tangibility departed, charmed her,
Embedded metempsychosis free
And easy matricide. Deeply, deeply
In our nature lies the octave, swarmed blur,
Celestial habitation of the bless't.
Prototypes of thy sanctuary rest,
That Aurelian inner citadel best
Of primordial devices edged fit
With gold sulphuric eagle spirit
Of serpent mercury lost near it.

LXII. THERE IS NO YEAR, BUT GENERATIVE LULL

Welded to assemblies of the next realm,
Vexillum with oriflamme break dividends,
Marlowe's Lucan and darkness my only friends,
Here at the southern transept window's helm,
at Dream-Story Chartres. God overwhelms
Violence and myth, regeneration's bends,
Belonging to that survivor who sends
His fittest song, lightning that splinters elms.
Take this bread in the wilderness freeing,
Pocket thy ancient constellation myths,
Lurid mills of alchemical blacksmiths.
Myths are dangerous not because they are,
But because reality is being,
Being survival of the fittest star.

LXIII. THE VIRTUE OF HYPOCRISY

Recall the poetic order's excess,
Harsh tempests of chronology abound,
Branch and soil, convent and diocese grounds,
Peculiar relevance beyond redressed
Realms of abstract speculation's confessed
Polarities of revolt's grace abound,
Reflective influence, fury and sound,
Thucydidean rivals Romanesque.
Powerlessness is strength made perceptive,
Expectancy the new destination,
That which the profane all do, I do not,
for I have seen horror's face abjective,
Jurisdictions of annihilation,
Far from the west façade, narthex's lot.

LXIV. WE WERE STRANGERS FOR A TIME, UNTIL DEATH

Protracted its charge, split Vulcan machine.
O Ioannes Cassianus green
With Egyptian crucifix, shortened breath,
Passing through the alleys of whoredom's meth,
Monks who steadfastly make thy worn soul *clean*,
Plant lives of animals relinquished mean
The pyramidal hour narrows, Macbeth
Seeking stricter self-extinction's boned leth,
To convey the gift in this recurrence,
Of time's assassin I gave to all saints,
The wine-rinsed mystery of redemption,
Lodge-blue cognate walls of the exemption,
Exteriors shaded with pearl grey paints,
Thomas Tallis, hymnal reassurance.

LXV. SPEAK OF MOUNTAINS, MY LOVE, THE CALL OF THINGS

(*Regnum meum non est de hoc mundo*)

Unto this last, angel the die is cast,
Serenity now life in the spirit;
Unto this last, the past not even past,
Angels shall sing, and we shall hear it.
The age is indeed paradise lost,
The wine of youth unto winter frost.
The hour is now well spent
Who shall be saved? Who shall repent?
Unto this last, a light doth shine,
Into thy heart. Seek ye Heaven fine,
Witness the evil one withering depart.
There was none beside me in the end but Him,
Grace's interior light to comprehend—
Thou shalt be saved, if ye endure to the end.

LXVI. THE FALL OF PURGATORY FRAMES PITTANCE

Still my walled Bacchae landscape underscores,
Architecture-skeletons with kettles,
Compositional designs, stone metal,
Armatures of martyrs, embedded doors,
Responds frail without bracing arcade floors,
Galleries, tympana, flower petals,
Colonnettes membrane-thin. Once unsettled,
Concealment's true volume cast like die stored,
To cross-ribbed frail bundles of soaring shafts.
Symbol t'ward the kingdom of God on earth,
Transcending all other concerns of life,
Into its physical dimensions graphed,
Mere slits, living bones of tower-crowns birthed,
I am in here, some water with its knife.

LXVII. METAPHYSICS OF ABSOLUTE NEGATIVITY

Metaphysical negativity,
Virgin breastmilk for Saint Bernard,
Updates on this, some absolute canard,
Confessions make the virgin's sealed heart free.
Science has nothing to say to paint, see,
Byzantine mosaic draped with cords, hard
Portraitures for robots, martyrs, whores, bard,
All save lantern light, I, and my chimney.
Stand, clap, this curtsy's metaphysics of
Absolute negativity sings low,
Assignments wrecked, insane and poor and free,
One and many shall venerate the dove.
She cheats on solitude with sleeping. Woe
To sanity! Give my dreams back to me!

LXVIII. JOHN SENIOR'S MASS ORNAMENT

Baths of Diocletian, where clothlike flesh
Glistened in whisper, meditation skull
In hand at towers of the façade full
Of old masters, lest broken frames enmeshed
Set down candles for all-night vigil fresh
With chorale lauds and wreaths of smoke that pull
That nocturnal bather's still golden wool,
Into algebraic firmament threshed.
At least a shadow of the masterpiece,
Towers of the façade at Hell's season,
Haltingly reconvened, the marble die
Cast before beaded statues that release
This parliament of fools from pure reason,
Headless politicians laughing through rye.

LXIX. RESURRECTION'S SOLEMN MUSIC

His distorted tin of some human molars
Far from the objective-correlating crowd.
Immersion in the infinite ocean's solar,
Eternal light, classless Elysian fields ploughed,
Heiress to the holy cult of beads endowed.
Like Anastasios the Librarian,
I second that compleinte (Chaucerians bowed).
I, Denis Carthusian, contrarian,
Summon magnetic mountains' agrarians,
Dissector of the insufficient nations,
Drury Lane, Grub Street, and rambling Marians,
Troubadours sprinkled ash, lavender plantation,
"That life is death, heaven's reality throes
"Pierced by perpetual rows of windows."

LXX. THE CLOCK OF BLOOD

Young Bruno, patching dilapidated
Parts of the old schoolroom building's window,
Cinnamon shop on his mind, rescinds though,
Benedictine labor celebrated,
As processed edification drawn slated,
Sanctified the soul, this future shrine shows,
The church is fractal without grace split throes,
Wallpaper wakes of pierced horizon fated,
Illuminates this builder's intellect,
Angelic hosts in heaven & mirth,
His rich moral artistic powers fit,
Coterie of ghettos where I reflect,
When we discovered what is called the earth,
And decided that we didn't like it.

LXXI. SWEET LADY BREAKING STONES, ARMED WITH MADNESS

The forest wardens called in from abroad
Masons, artists, to the Gate of the Sun,
Where carpenters and stained-glass painters awed,
At Hagia Sophia with the One,
The arch of Orion, like midnight runs,
Into the fragrance of neglect. Seven
Candlesticks' odorous sound, light begun,
Sought, with fulmination's bread unleavened,
Magical stabilities of Heaven.
Goldsmiths, sculptors, at the Gate of the Moon,
Tabernacle curtains all eleven,
To condemn the world, let it perish soon,
Who seek light and permanence in earnest,
Having been put through the fiery furnace.

LXXII. OBLIVION IS MY HOST AND ALTAR

I hath been terribly misunderstood
Here in Gloucester, fishing rod, cough, canned worms,
This concern expected something more firm,
A millionaire with news that is good.
But I don't know, at station, if I should
Let it go, proceed up to BC's burnt
Croker and gold pot, nunnery learned
In ways of television-thinking (would
Nail into the mind of this free spirit),
All these emotional thoughts right near it,
The subject of the talks: stuttering drunk
Cleric who could not keep quiet, ten trunks
Books nobody understands, reading games,
Alas the same in difference; the same.

LXXIII. EVOLUTION AND CONVERSION

The real wise man's an idiot & the real
idiot is wise, e'en president or king,
One down at abandoned bus stop's rubber ring,
Alone in pouring rain Latinity's seal,
Memories of the monastery reveal,
For once in her life, she was happy, poor thing,
Plastique façade flanked by two towers that sings,
Disintegration is security's weal,
Deposit neither heart nor trust in apes,
Instead, ambulatory crown of chapels,
Messages of light through those most sacred windows,
Be like for body and soul a quilt a cape,
Opacity then contraction quake apple
Carts ample, and this bedmaker's rescind thro.

LXXIV. HER STONE FEET OF INSOMNIAC DREAMS AND

Sacked sonority, thought of flavor,
In search of timber, self-reliant men,
Prayers are not answered, the truth I gave her,
For if they were one could stop saying them.
The surest bet is ambiguous phlegm,
Or predetermined tablet declension.
My good friend, the raving shoemaker Behme's
Surplus variations on ascension
Exile, mayhem, death is prophet's pension.
Immediately available those
Models that gave free reign to invention,
Suger's whole imagination disclosed,
Trotting down Point Reyes vast steps and rungs,
Boulder fleeced with cloudlike cotton dung.

LXXIV. HEARSES (WINTER)

Science is but religion's stillborn bead,
Without precedence or parallel need,
Use of light, the unique relationship,
Between structure and appearance equipped,
With the wake of webbed consolidation,
Expansion's clerestory zone stationed,
Through reduction of inert surfaces
Rapacious feudatories, earth that is,
Concerned with pleasant problems of design,
Composition's concern is most sublime,
The idea of an icon in stone,
Integration of architecture's throne,
Sculpture human figure doth merge rigid,
Pattern columned archivolts made frigid.

LXXV. *CIRCUITOUS ORATORIORUM*

Now mine own grandeur disobedience,
Hath sent me falling from the perisht sky,
Where senses overcome collapse & I,
Prescribe regicide for that coiled wince
Of democratic princes. Ever since,
Symphonies of utopian undried
Guillotines, sons of the father of lies,
Against all souls who torture babes evinced,
Devoured saturnine, delirious
Inversion's atom-crushing kind that tears
Worlds in two. Unlade mariners prepared,
Through Leviathan's most imperious
Mental chains, the same author, God himself,
His guidance stocks the solar faith's bookshelf.

LXXVI. BLACK HOUSE

If not soil drenched with blood, then mental war
It shall be. War is being, though spirit
Yearns temporally forever near it,
With the king of kings. Witness Mary soar
As the Seat of Wisdom, her mindless whores,
Droning souls the living gone, their clear slit
Of memorization lodged means that seared pit
In bent degraded heads, their vented cords,
Mutilated wizardry of finance.
War music, drum-taps, harshest sentence saved
For one who dares from throne of righteousness
Allude to truth. I turn to eight saints glance
At faces of the pillars of the nave,
Memorize with love-codes' licentiousness.

LXXVII. EVERYTHING OUTSIDE THE SOUL IS NOTHING

Steadfast protection of obscurity,
Just as the nest is built into the bird,
The die is cast, possession fast yearns for thee,
At last, there was the beauty of the Word.
Truth's deracination, solar faith heard,
So when the evil one takes all its gall,
Preaching clerics with their meanings nigh blurred,
Life becomes hollow in the sacred hall,
Of eternity's gates, and gods who fall.
Narcotized masses, disgrace to ascetics,
Meanwhile you cannot speak the truth at all,
Pigsty masturbation homiletics.
Bucolic tray of cloves whole & crushed,
I'll cast forth first stone, though I'm in no rush.

LXXVIII. ON THE OCCASION OF READING WILLIAM PENN'S PREFACE TO GEORGE FOX AT SUNSET IN A CAB FROM CITY HALL TO THE UNIVERSITY OF PENNSYLVANIA

Posterity makes sense of everything,
Explains all, and thus it explains nothing,
Unless one willing to approach and ring
Around economic vocal cords, sing
A new song of convenience for the Lord.
No doubt the voters' minds like corpses swing
In the death of ecstasy's due accord,
Embark hallucinatory progress,
Oracles permanently see restored
Hegelian writing on the wall abscessed,
That we learn from history that we do
not learn from history (fanged opalesce).
Religions, limited eternities,
Are geographic sensibilities.

LXXIX. TRAHERNE INTERLUDE (STONES OF FIRE FALLING FROM THE SKY)

Equilibrium lost on all but thee,
Singing neath vaulted sky of genesis,
Mute strings of chamber-memory,
That wax mahogany holds ether sea,
Stab southward with Michael at Nemesis,
Refusals to mourn, to let it be,
Weapons of another democratic,
Mutilation, that hyperemesis,
Of collective delusion's memory,
Courage to face chaos sultry static—
But our sign liberates, it knows, makes free.

LXXX. NOT ONLY THE AUTHOR OF VISIBILITY IN ALL VISIBLE THINGS BUT GENERATION & NOURISHMENT & GROWTH

I have no doubt their minds have been destroyed,
For they were never forced into this plight.
Light is the creative principle joy
in all things; they hate nothing more than light.
The objective value of any thing
Is determined by the degree to which
It partakes of light. Doth it love, or sing?
Doth it take to wound with charity's stitch?
Divine line penetrates the universe
According to its own ring'd dignity
Take the Republic from my maiden's purse
And turn to book six: here the good we see
Is defined as the cause of knowledge right:
Being and essence, compared to sunlight.

LXXXI. STORMING SOLICITATION'S CIRCUMSTANCE

Liturgical vessels and furniture cast,
Resplendent with both gold and precious stones,
What I would have given, to relinquish,
The customary, its sick vast hallowed,
Machinations against the age steadfast.
Its aim to kill reason itself enthroned,
Papers prayers cast into ceramic dish,
An altar made in part by glass gallows,
Merciful eyes of solitudes past.
I no longer recognize the sky's dome–
What time doth the sun die? The moon cry's wish?
Nethermost sediment in her mental shallows,
Brackish calumniators, celestial intimacies,
Her last pride, to live in his memory.

LXXXII. CONCEPTUAL REBIRTH FROM INTELLECT

Neither heartbreaking nor staggering but
Anencephalous. Guttural placid
Ethics, morals, utopian acid,
Free gifts of posterity logic's rut,
Which any fool can garner pillage gut,
In the name of pilled Alcools, Mass did
Its nonexistent justice, myth placid.
Symmetry's sea, regeneration's soot
Go verily to fittest survivors.
In beholding this light, we revive her,
Resurrected submersion in matter,
Irregular bays and narrow ladders,
Plagued obstacles confront the pioneer,
Discontented subjection, solemn veneer.

LXXXIII. SHE BREAKS THROUGH INTO THE REALM OF ESSENCE

Verticalism reverses movement
Of gravity, that House of God no pale
Commonplace, but long petrifying bent
Shallow segmental shells and hand-carved sails.
Those were my last gothic sanctuaries,
Spherical outer walls, lost crates of ale.
She established with pink beam a merry
Textual cathedral, empirical
Façade for sacred interiors buried,
Inside of her, where my desire burns full,
Spreads, envelopes. Our metaphysical
System turns torturous course, angels lull,
My angel takes me from the frozen sea,
Come closer, by rung and rope, enter me.

LXXXIV. SUGER'S CONSECRATION CEREMONY

Why the dross migraine of revolution,
That historical constellation heeds,
Whereby fact is fiction, fiction fact's seed.
Pictorial rhetoric's solution,
The portal's mental electrocution,
Colonne borne of Cistercian book like Bede,
Illumination statue-still, the Creed's
Square bays, side aisles, arcade evolution,
of the Gate of Dawn's Light of Patriarchs,
For whom there were two options: insanity
Abject, Sacrosanct filth, whilst afraid he
Beheld greatest moment in history,
Broken bread, barndoor delivery's arch,
Do this, he said, in memory of Me.

LXXXV. SOLITUDE DEPOSED, ITS BRITTLE GLORY

I kneel, remember sleepwalking across
October tile, ratiocination,
I see unfold the mystical vision
Of harmony that the divine reason
Established through cosmos of gilded dross.
Equilateral triangle stations
Square, triangle, that prevail, collisions
Of thought stacked in volumes vast as seasons.
Guibert of Nogent, golden section moss
Of Euclid—this lost and found vibration,
Austere its subordination, decisions
Of the human figure made to please Him.
Holy architecture of prayer, perish't strife:
To pass more confidently out of this life.

LXXXIV. THE DANCING HORSE OF PANDEMONIUM

Historiography is an instrument
Of politics, that torn allegories
At quadrivium made me repent.
Bocaccio and I exchanged stories,
At the Portal of the Incarnation,
Exile, mania, and other glories.
Chaplet weavers, the weight of creation,
Members of Platonic academy,
Come and see ecstasy of the stations,
O angel, wilt thou say a prayer for me?
Christ portrayed within central tympanum,
Choir of angels, saints in concert for thee.
O heavenly thy hierarchy's sea,
                    Dionysian luminosity.

LXXXV.

What is, you ask, this illusionistic
Image of the Celestial City,
Everywhere the invisible reflects
Invisible, symbolic wilderness,
Of the world of appearances whose wick
Ne'er goes out. Bright, bright, is vanquished pity,
That which is brightly coupled with connects
With thy bright principle's reduced surface.
Keys to the unquenched fire of love come quick,
All or nothing when the vision hit thee,
Winter is Death, Spring is Life, God erects
The polished altar, pluming with incense.
Because the spirit departeth I weep,
Thou, my shepherd: I shall not want or keep.

LXXXVI. LIMN DUST DOTH IN FACT DESTROY THE DIAMOND

We cannot from the mortal sin of cheap
Historical neglect deduce a thing.
Look at Milton's Eve: poor ideas seep,
Generations point the finger and ring,
Without rigorous investigation.
The mythological snake somehow sings,
Causality is her destination,
Not the stars. That irreversible move
Was so human it begs vindication,
Eve was prepared to blame, never improve,
Everyone, everything, except herself,
The hopscotch of blame keeps apes on the move.
I do not blame her for this wild solar malaise;
Tis her maker who's in fact a little crazed.

LXXXVII. DOS PESOS [TAVERN INTERLUDE]

Against history as limp history,
Beholden to locked ideology,
For ideology doth hateth most
Reality, golem scribes, eyes of clay,
Fearing offense, we promulgate decay,
Turn temporal lust into a new Host,
Machinations dissolve dichotomies,
Rape of the mind just cosmic whist to thee.
Calls for unity just more suppression,
Vergil and Machiavelli, whist a-gain,
Face value is castrated intercourse,
Pacifism is social succession,
Through recurring degeneration's plain,
Crushing truth by sheer suicidal force,
Charlatans tilt the unclean cup to blur,
Shake thy spear, I and God be murderers.

LXXXVIII. INTERIOR CATHEDRAL

The cathedral was designed as an image,
Transparent diaphanous connects cold dusk's
Ambulant galleria, the choir's chapel,
At polished archivolts rather than along
Geometric jambs of church portal belong
There with figures of the virgins in papal
Frame of the abbot's portal, sifting smoke husks,
Baptismal font's story of a soul's tillage,
Michelangelo's vision, the hermitage
Within, Adamic hand oblivion's tusk,
Permanently near, combat's divine grapple,
Permanently out of reach, designer's psalm,
Mechanistic alchemy made real presence,
Indivisible foundation and essence.

LXXXIX. FANTASIA ON PSALM 69:20

Set the house of neutrality ablaze,
Colliding wickers, Wilting hollow men,
Render me a prophet against empire,
Solomonic Temple canst now descend.
A compensation for what he had not
Himself seen coming, blinded by decay,
As the invisible noose it tightened,
Desecrating form to ashen gray.
Bondage's discovery, quartermaster
Drinking rubied alley port, but faster,
Mutable cosmos that fit in one's throat,
Twelve propagandists burnt inside the mote.
Everything is coming down. Don't look back—
No victors had, nor counterattack.

XC.

Before cabinet of breadless art,
He stands swallowing blue. Please pray for him!
Neglected lecterns bring light to the dim
Homogeneity among all parts
Of the edifice. Vaults in ashlar start
To tremble with dressed stone, each preserved limb,
A vision of durability's hymn,
Against the dying of the day apart
From the madding crowd. His house has many
Mansions, for he who would endure the last
Temporal triumphant beast's passages,
Those evaporated assuages.
He stands against the Beast System uncanny,
There 'tis, the age's end, approaching fast.

XCI.

Retain dominance, control you proclaim
To disdain through lifelong Feste reversed,
Theatrical self-hatred's phlegm thy purse.
The physical world as it's known, insane,
Has no reality but symbol, stained
Definitions and some perceptive curse.
Splendor Veritatis, I sang, to burst
Upon language-death of Being, strained,
Rebuilders of the calling-out, ontic-
vision and disclosure, mine own private
Secular resurrection. Sing, sinners,
Who ceased war against the idols, tis brick
& mortar themselves that spurned up twilit
Chaos, wrath, otiose city dinners.

XCII. LIKE UNTO TH' SYNDICATE OF YEARNING

Gothic architecture is symbol,
Of supernatural reality,
Representation's relative darkness,
Sending back quicksilver for electrum.
At bitter technological cliff full
Of psychic volcanos' capacity,
With Domesday Book, Blake's "Milton" & starkness
Scarred hands of locusts, wild honey's spectrum,
Christian Hermeticism that thimble
Even Balthazar lauds, his fealty
Safe in pregnant vaults where Vaughan's larks still guess
Theophilus of Edessa's plectrum,
Adrienne Speyr's dwelling bedpan visions,
Croon Greek astrological tradition.

XCIII. DIGITAL FEUDALISM (STRAW FOR THE FIRE THAT YE SHALL COME AND SEE)

The cosmic temple's ornament as thine own,
Order's interior disharmony,
Tectonic function chain'd and knit enthroned,

Gather subtle chains for this ring of bone.
Herein anthologized torture devices,
Lie like satanic cloth, mountains of drones,

Statical measuring rod suffices,
The mason's stone ax, black sun collision,
Face set like flint, double-bind entices,

Boethian geometry's vision,
Geometrical submission profound,
Medieval dungeon table incisions,

Neutral parties, said the angel, are bound,
For the darkest pits of Hell's screaming grounds.

XCIV. PETROS EREMITE

O Peter! How ye fare all mad journey
Crucifying heretics, burning straw,
Cemeteries consecrated to law
And love, and something about stars' gurney,
With satchel, strap, hook and crook, ye learn thee
Smoldering minarets choking them raw,
Butchers and heretics deserve the saw,
Zodiacal trial by fire. Now turn, see
Thy knights on horseback thundering inward
Down the wretched mountain, necklace fountains
Fill the cups of a jewel's crusaded stage,
Wooden trim for chapel and vast vineyard.
Burning calligraphy, one made free—sin
Extinguished in heirloom smokestacks of rage.

XCV. POSSESSION

Jacob had twelve sons and yet loved just one.
And as for me, yes madame, ystruly,
I say to Hell with positivity.
We overturn testaments to the sun,
Deception's ladder, wishing well done
Up with illuminatively poor seas,
Desolate lands and severed hands, the key,
Indolent moors, wild horses on the run.
Quantity incidental then as now,
Behold the clerics bowing to golden cows,
These bovine minds endowed with nothing real,
Ne'er profound; let them neither lead nor steal,
I and mine after Jacob's Ladder;
Diogenes intact, nothing madder.

XCVI. VESTIGES OF DIVINITY

She just can't be happy today, one just
Must let the body be: let it form, let
It break, let it make mother scream, yet
These screams be sounds of Being for they must.
Grow and whisper yes, whisper no, break rust
Chains with the water of thy youth: Regret
Little but breath, the dust of this planet,
Where the bodies multiply-cry-die-trust.
Let the body split, let it sift and sleep,
Let it burn, let it suffer, let it weep.
Let the body not exist, let a tryst
Be a tryst, let those glassy eyes that wish
For the impossible fall apart. Let
Them go unto the sacred fount and yet—

XCVII. SACRED CHARADES

Technology and ontic death eclipse
He whose best friends are hallucinations
Nor more in life might that be a station,
Burn his holy books, pry open his lips.
Summoned to Manchester, sullen the drips
He swallowed like ratiocination,
Leviathan in mourning, strange ways win
Out despite the crowd's incessant cries slip
Into the first commandment's frozen lake.
Progress's victims burnt at brand new stakes,
To perennial chants, starvation takes
Its hands on the controls of confidence.
Sonorous cadence, optimism rents
One last room to a more occult past tense.

XCVIII. STIGMATA (TO CATALOGUE THE DAY'S DEFICIENCIES)

Smooth goatee of pestilence fair auburn
in his shrinking prison cell. Moonlit mice
provide the single grotesque sounds, jaw turned
in spastic memory of absinthe, lice,
gunfire, the scent of paper burning nice
and fresh. Vacant aids' courtyard's crow caws, yearns,
for unpicked bones, like in thought he saw learned
men begging him to be still—but the price
of debauched pleasure is too good. That crowd's
laughter's stony air of cindered moss smote
structured temporality—One allowed
too much noise on the way to silence, quotes
biblical begin to burn his eyes. Now
God alone dwells in this stone cell remote.

XCIX. THE GLEANERS: VARIATIONS ON A PAINTING

Distant stand the emotive dispossessed,
Far from blistered fingertips and torn dress,
Of gleaners sanctified by sacral time,
Adorning their interior sublime.
Come freezing rain, rectangular despair,
Father Louis, Odysseus repair,
Sirens of salt, leaping my arms outspread,
Set on the reappearance of the dead.
The crumbs of love of ye the late living,
Italian Market dusk, vistas giving
Forth cup, plate, tray, glance, word, all the light
And aura of persistence calm aright.
We do not recall the moguls grim,
But we doth love forever plainclothes cherubim.

C. WAITING FOR THE LORD

My Lord God, beyond language in earnest,
How I waited for Thou in my sorrow,
I thought I knew all, thus nothing furnished
Made foundations in my heart's tomorrow,
In learning to pray not for things, but Thou,
For Your presence in my heart forever,
I knew not when nor where, nor why, nor how,
That I might doubt Thy Will not, nigh, never.
Through bread and wine, thy Triune Spirit flows,
The living bones of sacred mystery,
My Lord God, beyond comprehension still,
Illuminate we who stand and wait close
To You in prayerful love's epiphany,
In waiting here, according to Thy Will.

Babylonian Odes, & Whispers of Gomorrah:

An Epilogue for Stage

JOHN CLARE'S BLUES

O minister my prostitute, lying
through your teeth! Thy ministry is cheap grace,
Cupertino sees sin-filth on thy face,
This minister, my prostitute's mind dying.
The carnal sermons are so poor, prying,
That ye hold no candle to the whore's lace,
Like spider web lodgings ye made this case,
O minister my prostitute. Crying,
A portly sheep adorned in wolf's clothing,
Political theologies he'd sing!
Along with bloody Sunday came the cash,
Whence pharmakoi sideswept his vision brash,
The Hell ye preached is now all thine, alas,
"Ay Satan, thou canst kiss my fucking ass!"

TWENTY-SEVEN WAGONS FULL OF SALT PILLAR FRAGMENTS

I see thy nipples standing in the sun,
Little magnetic exclamation points,
Forgotten silk, a cup of milk, fair air
Gone brisk inoculates my winter brain.
My heart is hanged; a crescent made of coins
Breaks apart, one by one into the sea
They glitteringly ripple whilst the balm
Of consecration brings thine eyes to mine.
And lo! Ye smile sweetly through bead of sweat
Lady in white, niggardly absconded
Petrified by thy quenching pink arrows
Divine prototype of gemination
Yesterday you were seated, looking plain,
Ahead, not up; today it is my turn.

IN ITS SHADOWS INSECTS SCRAMBLE RUSHING

The Freedom Tower is but a syringe,
A symbol of the future's composure.
Behold! Apocalyptic composers
Ventriloquize robots, and still yet winge
When the hollow corpses falter and cringe
With pangs of nullified rebirth, closure
Of an arcane school before bulldozer,
Through preset microscopic rubble singed.
Ceremonies within ceremonies
Erect testaments to obfuscation,
Where once plurality conveyed fresh air.
To the inverted palace of nowhere,
Holocaust's recurring consecration,
Strikes terror in plebeian rooms of hair.

THE MURAL OF CRUELTY

The more murals unveiled, said the lady,
The more violence there is, like Hades,
Hath been unleashed here in thy lost city.
O sirens, ugly paintings, a pity
I tell you. Profane collage of winsome
Delusions, fatherless boys at gin-drums,
Monomania for exterior
Rots the soul. The renegade professor
said to me, "All their art's inferior,
"Murals everywhere but so is trash", slurred,
"At the range, no more fear of the tactless,
"Sue Sontag's face became bullseye practice.
"One needn't believe in the soul, I say,
"Tho this maketh not the soul go away."

HERE COMES SHOWTIME THE TWERKING RABBI

Life, at best, is a grotesque mistake,
And at its worst terminates in a fiery lake;
So the next time elated, belatedly high,
Remember soon you'll come down,
And later still, die.
The sooner you learn that there's nothing to cherish,
The better you'll feel when the time comes to perish.
For the high point of life is in sitting quite still,
While the bottles and bodies make you stupid and ill.
Love thy enemies, and take stock in feeling blue;
Sanhedrin adrift, without further ado,
Tis his turn to die of the seasonal flu.

ENCEPHALOPATHY

Guns, rights, barbarians:
The mob relies upon assumption.
Innocents, fascism, invasion:
Assumption is based on inexperience.
Pharmaceutical minds, guiding
Drugged, brainwashed fools, falling
For anything that promises to allure.
Don't worry about that professor:
She's a professional liar.
Here, the truck keys: bring thy
Psychoanalytic couch to the fire.
Destruction works best from within;
Yet who can endure stupidity for that long?
Thou art right to concede
That something is in fact wrong.

OUTSIDE THE BASILICA I HEARD IT SAID, 'HATE YOUR NEIGHBOR AS YOU HATE YOURSELF'

Impenetrable nature of matter,
Receiving its visual existence,
From an energy that doth transcend it,
Lyre psalmodies of Orphic insistence,
Stained-glass window denies the lies that bind,
Plato's theological persistence.
I was there at Bruno's trial, type and kind,
Siphon and straw, the fury and the sound,
Bronze melted to beads, wrapped around the mind,
Poet can't be destroyed and must confound,
Boxed ash, the weight of oblivion,
Interior prisons become profound,
God's death is old news for they who fill pews—
Triumphant therapeutic's scattered clues.

THE LATE SUMMER MARKET

The church bells breathe into that turning heel,
Somewhere within the air of carnival,
A child squealing unseen from that stroller,
Christian's pillars Anthony, Lorenzo,
Something softer than gray-pink envelopes,
I ought to retrieve Werner's nomenclature,
If not for the dusk market calling me.

The butcher's somehow always understaffed,
Which works out just fine in the dusty end,
Here where the generations framed keep watch,
Over time, the river, gelati cups,
The comedy of divinity stalls,
Dressed in revolting garments, mismatched shoes,
Lumbering back to the prophetic not-here.

It is the sky above the dusk Market,
Too good for photograph or video,
Here at old Christian and Ninth looking south,
Portal to beatific sanity,
To watch all of the temporal way,
Veined leaves set into vast swirl a-knocking,
Thoughts like comets, café, zenith & prayer.

The old man with newspaper was just born,
Living scriptures at the hour of our death,
That waft of pipe smoke pricks up his good ear,

Saturnalia in the sunlit section,
Roped off for the famished women and men,
Who yesterday were running through blacktop,
To the radiance of their mother's arms.

That Italian Market sky operates,
In ways that resurrect Platonic Forms,
Bringing solace to the broken-hearted,
Resurrection of the artist's deep heart,
Her canopies unveil reason itself,
Walking blistered miles toward the town of life,
Checking the ember locket's good intact.

In the split space of one turning to go,
Toward knowing we're all phantoms of ourselves,
Cherubic wanderers resume movement,
Church bells ringing out through chorus voices,
The Muses guide me gently by the hand,
From the eternity of the present,
Into the blessed solitude of night.

TRACES OF THE BEAST

Moloch's child hath poet as priest though
I am Dionysius, first rank
After the holy Apostles,
Corpus areopagiticum.

Traces of the beast, in every glance,
Save the righteous eyes like glittering jewels;
Traces of the beast, withered askance,
In exile sacred, sharing our tools.

I am a slave of solitude,
Nocturnal tears, a soul dimly hued.

Deus culpa,
I must be still, though;
Deus culpa,
I must know.

Traces of the beast, it to come,
This is close enough for me.
Traces of the beast, it hath been done,
This satanic epic snatches up
The ones once free.

Shadow has become reality:
I would know, He leadeth me.

*Deus culp*a,
I must be still, though
Deus culpa,
I must know.

Lord, I must know.

www.ingramcontent.com/pod-product-compliance
Lightning Source LLC
LaVergne TN
LVHW051647080426
835511LV00016B/2542